What I've Learnt in Lockdown

in Lockdown

Following the 'Rules' for Togetherness

Illustrations by Lyn Halvorsen

Chris Mellor

ISBN: 978-1-9995810-4-6

First published 2021

Introduction

To understand where 'What I've Learnt in Lockdown' came from, it is right for me to give due credit to my inspiration.

When we first went into lockdown on Monday 23rd of March 2020, a memorable day for many reasons, I took it upon myself to send my eighty or so work colleagues, all now working from home, a nugget of humour, a joke, or perhaps a video at 3.30pm every afternoon. I soon noticed I had many notifications, and material, some unsuitable, pouring in to my many WhatsApp groups and that my colleagues were appreciating something humorous popping up in their inboxes every afternoon.

Over time, this morphed into something bigger. I added multiple features, and included subjects such as 'Quotation of the day,' 'Smile of the day,' 'Wine of the day,' 'Joke of the day' and even 'Lego of the day,' to name but a few. It also started to include: 'I've learnt...'

So where did this feature come from?

Well, one day in a WhatsApp chat group, up popped, "I've Learned." A beautiful poem attributed to a man called Andy Rooney. Google it.

I did some research and discovered Andrew Aitken Rooney[1], to be an American radio and television writer best known for his weekly broadcast, entitled, 'A Few Minutes With

Andy Rooney'. This was a part of the C.B.S. News program 60 Minutes from 1978 to 2011. His final regular appearance on 60 Minutes aired on October 2, 2011. He died a month later, at the age of 92.

Andy Rooney was a man who had the gift of saying so much with so few words. I adored his poem and started to share a line a day with my colleagues.

After about six weeks, I had almost run out of material for the daily feature, but it occurred to me over one weekend that I had been involved in quite a few personal 'I've learnt' moments and incidences during lockdown, and witnessed a few, some of which required action on my part to keep my marriage on an even keel. I felt it might be a good idea to write some of these down, and use them to keep up the daily bulletins. Once I started, one or two of my colleagues even sent me details of their own experiences, which I could then put into words.

I am sure that if you are reading this, you may well relate to some of these passages and also see the funny side. You may even have experienced some yourself!

So here is 'What I've Learnt in Lockdown...,' featuring the passages which were published as part of my daily bulletin to my work colleagues. One or two have been edited and tidied up, but the original thought remains.

What I have truly learnt during lockdown has, I hope, made me a better person, and along the way, my wife and I have had many laughs, and the odd cross word! I also learnt, that if in the wrong, it is always better to apologise afterwards.

Please enjoy the following, and have a quiet grin as I do when re-reading them. I am still writing new passages down.

Chris.

To my darling wife Karen

After 37 years
we still make each other laugh.

Thank you.

Contents

Everything Happens in the Kitchen...............1

The Food of Love.. 6

Keeping It Clean 18

Personal Care..28

Housekeeping, Gardening and Dogs............34

Harmony in the Bedroom.............................46

Work and Hobbies 52

Christmas etc...60

Wise Words...66

Everything

Happens

in the Kitchen...

I've learnt...

...That the blue cloth used for wiping down kitchen surfaces and worktops:

a) Lives in the grey box by the kitchen sink,

b) Does NOT live in the lounge,

c) Should NOT be used to wipe floors,

d) Should be rinsed in hot water after use.

Furthermore...That I must not leave the blue cloth lying around and covered in tuna-mayonnaise. Subsequently, trying to say to my wife that it was not me will be met with incredulity, and it will be strongly pointed out that I have clearly just made and eaten a tuna-mayonnaise sandwich for lunch. The best option here, is to apologise, AGAIN, for a continually repeated offence, and offer to wash and clean the cloth.

...That being asked to do the washing-up (although if I am ahead of the game I shouldn't need to be asked), actually means using washing-up liquid and hot water.

...That to simply bring in the 100s of carrier bags of shopping from the porch to the kitchen is NOT ENOUGH. Without being asked, I need to automatically start putting the shopping away. Even putting items in the wrong place is better than not helping. If left in the bag, ice-cream melts.

...That if my wife gets up early to walk the dogs in the cooler part of the day, and on departing, shouts up and asks me to empty the dishwasher and make the bed, not to shout back that for me, it is a work day, and I am busy.

...That the fridge and freezer doors do not shut themselves. (Both the alarm and my wife will go off again and again and AGAIN!)

...That:

a) The dishwasher does not load itself.

b) If my wife has loaded the dishwasher I must not unload and reload it.

c) Equally, I most certainly must NOT re-organise my wife's loading of the dish-washer.

...That when I come downstairs from my office at 5.00pm and sit down at the kitchen island, my wife will say, whilst nodding at an offending plate covered in dried baked beans:
"You do know your plate from lunchtime is still there!"
I nod, knowing she is right, and that I have no answer.

...That when I say that I am taking the contents of the kitchen waste bin outside to the dustbin my wife will be appreciative.

The Food of

Love...

I've learnt…

…That if I put potatoes on to boil, it is not acceptable to leave them unattended and go and build Lego. The water will boil over resulting in raised voices and chastisement.

…That if I run out of milk in the morning, I should not expect the invisible 'Food Fairy' to have left a replacement carton in the refrigerator overnight. It would be better if I acknowledge when food is running out, and reorder online, or, better still, actually go to a supermarket, in person, on my own. Simply asking my wife where the fresh milk is will be answered with:
"I don't know, I don't drink milk." Followed by "How would you survive if you lived on your own?"

Still doesn't produce a new milk carton in the morning.

...That I must not be scared of going to the supermarket on my own, by myself, at least once.

...That when my wife is doing Pilates on Zoom, and I am therefore cooking dinner, it is not a good idea to interrupt her just to ask where the frozen peas are. Especially when she gets up, sighs, and goes to the freezer, only to locate them straight away.

...That if I require ketchup, I must check first to see if there is one already open in the fridge rather than just go to the larder and open a new one. That does not go down well. This rule also applies to any sauce, mayonnaise, salad dressing, thousand island dressing and the like.

...That if I use any liquids contained either in a bottle or carton and then put them back horizontally in the fridge, I must be sure that the lid is screwed on tightly. Failure to do so results in a sticky, dripping mess and the fallout from this is not something any healthy person should witness, and I am not talking fallout in the fridge.

...That if I am asked to cut up vegetables for a salad, I must check that I am using the oldest ones first. I will not be popular if I use those that were delivered that very morning.

...That if there is no bread at lunchtime and no-one has remembered to defrost a new loaf when they finished the last one, including me, it will be cheese on toast yet again.

...That if my wife has decided to attend a Tuesday evening yoga class outside her normal schedule, and I take it upon myself to prepare and cook the evening meal, (which should secure extra brownie points), accompanied by Chris de Burgh playing loudly on the speaker, I must focus on the cooking. Leaving the dirty potato saucepan on the draining board with the tap on, filling with hot water whilst I go back to my cooking, is not a good idea. My wife will throw up her hands in horror when greeted with torrents of hot, soapy water cascading over the draining board as she enters the kitchen at the end of her class. The dogs will look on incredulously and wonder what is going on, and the remainder of the evening will not be worth describing. Imagine my pain and discomfort!

...That when asked to prepare a salad, this consists of more than lettuce and one other vegetable. Four to five components are deemed to be acceptable by my wife.

...That if I cook the evening meal and then, for whatever reason, find myself singularly clearing up, loading the dishwasher, washing AND drying up because my wife is off doing something else, as the saying goes: 'Just Do It,' without a murmur. Life is too short, and I know everything equalises out. (I could always bring my hard work up at a later date, but this could well backfire on me....)

Similarly, ...That if I offer to cook the evening meal, this means just that. It means from start to finish, without being distracted. There is a right way of doing this! Cutting up vegetables, then sitting down, watching golf, being called back to garnish the fish, sitting down, watching golf, being called back to turn on the oven, sitting down, watching golf, being called back yet again to put the fish in the oven, will ultimately result in my wife getting exasperated and cooking the entire evening meal, which will then be eaten in total silence. However, I will be left with the clearing up which can be done in my own time, providing it is completed before bedtime. My wife will have retired to the lounge to watch television, leaving me to watch the golf in the study. Result!

...That when we buy kippers for me to make and cook kedgeree that evening, I need to look harder for the packet of turmeric which is essential to the dish, and which my wife has kindly left out for me right next to the recipe book, before doing her Pilates. I also need to wait until she has eaten and enjoyed her dinner before admitting I had failed to notice the necessary spice and had added a turmeric infused 'mocktail' teabag to the simmering rice instead.

...That if I am seeking to impress my wife as an aspiring Gordon Ramsey by cooking her a delicious raspberry soufflé, I must make sure I clear up everywhere afterwards, and then double check all surfaces. Otherwise, when my wife discovers smears of raspberry purée all over the sink, oven, fridge, recycling bin and bar stool, the result will be fallout and my efforts will go to waste.[2]

...That being totally honest in a relationship is not always the best and right decision. Sometimes, just sometimes, white lies are allowed between partners. So when my wife has spent hours standing and chopping vegetables, slaving to prepare a special vegan dish, and unbeknown to me, has backache and is tired and in need of help, sitting watching golf for hours by myself is rather inadvisable. Also inadvisable, is to declare the meal a little tasteless when asked. The results of this I will leave to your imagination. I will just add that three days after said incident life slowly returned to normal and I had learnt a major lesson. White lies are allowed and never relent on them. Take your private thoughts on certain subjects to your grave. White lies include: 'I love the new throw on the bed' and 'I really like your hair'.

...That my wife does accept and agree that I am very good at opening a bottle of wine, usually Rioja, at the right time each evening and then serving it perfectly aerated, filtered and at the correct temperature. I have also found that a surprise bottle of pink fizz usually helps the evening go very well.

Keeping It Clean...

I've learnt…

…That I have learnt a lot, an AWFUL lot, about washing clothes and hanging them out to dry.

…That like the dishwasher, the washing machine does not fill itself. Clothes do not magically move from the linen basket to the washing machine. SOMEONE must move them!

…That if I fill and use the washing machine, then I must also empty it.

…That I must not forget to add washing powder to the machine before starting a wash cycle. Clothes clean better that way.

...That the daily wash does not operate on one setting only. It can be changed to suit the required wash cycle. I did not know this. Thus, if my wife has used a 60 degree cycle previously, this may not be recommended for washing golf shirts. Shrinkage may well occur. And does.

…That when my wife shouts out:

"The tumble dryer is finished" it is her special code, and clear instruction for me to immediately, without delay and without being sidetracked nor distracted, empty the tumble dryer, and carefully fold and lay out the contents in the airing cupboard.

…That pants and knickers only need one peg when hanging on the line. NOT two.

But …

…That when hanging out the washing, most items such as shirts, dresses, tops, require more than ONE peg, and that sheets should not be allowed to drag on the ground whilst hanging from the line. Also, if using a 'whirligig,' start from the innermost line and work outwards, not the other way round. This makes life easier and results in fewer raised voices. (Some people may not like the way their washing is hung on the line as they dislike noticeable peg indentations on their T-shirts. However, if this is mentioned they are likely to be told to "DO YOUR OWN BLOODY WASHING AND HANGING!")[3]

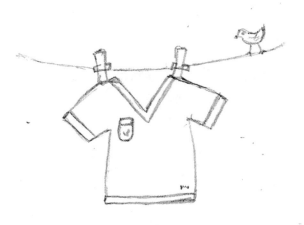

…That if I take responsibility for hanging out washing at 7.30pm, I must bring it in before bed. Leaving it out overnight results in it getting soaked with either dew or rain, and it may well need washing AGAIN. My wife will not be happy…

…That my wife appreciates it if I check that clothes are not inside out before hanging them, and also before placing them in the airing cupboard.

...That if I carefully fold my wife's wet jumpers after removing them from the washing machine without being asked, and place them all in the airing cupboard, my wife will pleasantly thank me. However, she will point out that I should not have piled all her jumpers one on top of the other. They should have been laid out separately.

...That clothes that go in the airing cupboard need to be folded, not thrown in. My wife can shout loudly when faced with an unruly pile of clothing in the cupboard.

...That pants, knickers and socks can just go in a pile in the airing cupboard. There is NO need to put socks in pairs. That really is OCD.

…That all clothes should not be washed together on the same temperature. There are different categories of clothes which should never be washed together, and then there are items such as 'delicates' which can shrink if washed at the wrong temperature in a job lot of washing. I did not know this. Getting this wrong can be very costly as new replacement clothing must be purchased at great expense.

…That it is not advisable to put very muddy, very soggy, pink gardening gloves in the washing machine without telling anyone. Someone else could come along and assume the machine is empty and proceed to wash their delicate white underwear. I must not even suggest that my wife should have checked that the washing machine was empty first as possible injury could ensue, plus a large bill on my credit card. Again!

...That "We have got grit in the airing cupboard!" actually means, "We have got Glis glis in the airing cupboard!" With my wife standing on a stool I must not suggest she moves the towels, as previously dormant Glis glis will spring to life and flee to the back of the airing cupboard. My wife will scream very loudly and almost fall off the stool into my arms, whereupon I bravely leap to catch her injuring myself in the process.

...That shirts need to be hung in the airing cupboard, but it is best to remember to check for Glis glis first, and always remember to shut the airing cupboard door after you. When my wife walks by and discovers it open...well....

...That if I lay a trap with a grape in it, I will catch a Glis glis.

Personal Care...

I've learnt...

...That I should always spray and wipe down the shower after use. Especially when asked to do so.

...That I should not use a clean hand towel to remove excess shaving foam from my face and then hang it back up. When discovered there will be a diplomatic incident.

...That if my wife and I are sharing a mirror, I do not trim my beard all over my wife's make-up bag as this could result in her face being adorned with flecks of beard trimmings when she applies her blusher, and our relationship could take a bad turn. The solution, of course, is to buy a second mirror. And possibly trim my beard outside...[4]

...That it is IMPERATIVE to squeeze the toothpaste tube from the bottom and not the middle. Squeezing anywhere other than the bottom will result in a loud verbal reaction from my wife. This equally applies to anything in a tube, ie, glue, hand cream, medication. You get the picture.

...That when my wife calls on her way home and asks me to run her some hot water with plenty of bubbles, I must remember she means in the bath and not the kitchen sink.

...That if I visit the bathroom at night to use the facilities, I must not put the main bedroom light on and I must avoid accidentally dropping the toilet lid as it may frighten my wife and cause her to leap out of bed. Either may result in being sent to the spare room for the rest of the night.

...That I must not walk through the front door after a Sunday meeting in a client's garden, with my face mask hanging off my thumb, and proceed to throw it to my wife and ask her to put it in the linen basket for me. As it falls to the floor, my wife will recoil and shout:

"DO IT YOURSELF!"

...That when my wife wakes up with a hangover, if, without being asked, I voluntarily do all the cleaning, washing, ironing, cooking and shopping that day, she will be most appreciative and recover more quickly.

Housekeeping,

Gardening

and Dogs...

I've learnt...

...That in some households there are pink jobs for ladies and blue jobs for gentleman. Some may say that blue jobs are not safe for ladies as they regularly require items such as either ladders, power tools or unsanitary conditions. Gentlemen should think carefully before attempting pink jobs for fear of breaking the washing machine and other essential equipment. [5]

...That outdoor shoes must be immediately removed upon entering the house. They must not be worn across a freshly cleaned and wet kitchen floor. Failing to keep to this rule will result in a death threat.

...That if I am merrily and happily working in the garden with the strimmer, I must not absent-mindedly strim my wife's favourite flower bed that she took hours planting out in the spring, and which are full of beautiful summer blooms. Nuclear fallout will occur and the strimmer may be used against me in a way that could affect my masculinity.

...That when washing a small dog in the Butler sink with the shower spray attachment, and with my wife in close proximity, I should not turn the spray on her in a jokey fashion. She will not find it as funny as me. The same applies when jet washing garden furniture.

...That, when is the toilet declared clean? Not after I have cleaned it if my wife's standards are anything to go by. I thought my standards were high enough. Obviously not, and this can be said about any of my cleaning skills.

...That when making the bed, my wife can both unbutton and button up the duvet cover much quicker than me. Why? I have no idea.

...That it is best to say:
"Yes, I will come," when asked to accompany my wife on a dog walk. This results in appreciation and happiness and works much better than my finding an excuse not to go.

...That it is imperative to thoroughly check any eBay order before pressing 'confirm and pay'. Lockdown has increased online ordering platforms such as eBay and Amazon. When ordering cans of antiperspirant, it is a good idea to check that when I order what I think is four cans, I have actually ordered four cans and not four packs of six cans, which means twenty-four cans of antiperspirant will be delivered and left towering on the doorstep.

...That 'Add to Basket' does not necessarily make me feel happier, but it will always make me just a bit poorer. [6]

...That all trees are sacred, especially those planted in our own garden by my wife. If I think that any such tree looks as if it requires a trim, it is advisable to check with my wife first. Failure to do this and cutting off either the wrong or too many branches, may result in the clippers being directed towards my own most prized 'branch,' with potential ramifications that are not worth contemplating.

...That my wife knows more if not everything, about our Wi-Fi operated central heating system. How is that? I have no idea but it is a godsend. This is fantastic, although I am stuffed if it goes wrong, and she is not at home! Maybe she should teach me how it works.

...That my wife has an issue with shoes that are not on my feet. If said shoes, or multiple pairs even, are left lying around, they will mysteriously disappear from the place I left them. I will need to search high and low for them when I need them, finally being forced to ask my wife where they are. This will result in the repeat of a long lecture about leaving shoes out, trip hazards, etc, and I will be reminded that all shoes should be tidied away when not in use, even though I will be wearing them again in an hour's time. Illogical.

Also...

...That when my wife is hoovering, and I am working hard in my office, the following words will reach me:

"I am having to move your shoes again. Shoes live in cupboards, not on the floor!"

...That it is best to turn the lights out when leaving a room. Always. It's as simple as that.

Life becomes a lot quieter and more peaceful when adhering to this rule.

...That when I say:

"Yes, I will do it," when asked by my wife to bring her wellington boots indoors from where she left them outside, it is a task that should be carried out straight away. Getting side-tracked and forgetting and therefore leaving her boots outside all night in a rainstorm does not bode well for the following day's dog walk, nor the rest of my day.

...That if I hear my drowned and sodden wife returning to the back door with two equally wet and sodden dogs after their morning walk, I must rush down from my office, and without being asked, open the back door and offer to hose down the dogs in the Butler sink. When my wife is inside, changed and dry, she will give me a big hug and a kiss by way of a thank-you.

Harmony in

the Bedroom...

I've learnt...

...That to make the first cup of tea of the day for my wife whilst she is still in bed, gets the day off to a good start for everyone.

...And that to make the second cup of tea of the day for my wife results in thanks, love and appreciation, and the rest of the day spent working from home is all the better for it.

...That if my wife is last out of bed and I pop back into the room to find the bed still unmade, I take the time to make it. It is the 'spur of the moment' little things that count in a relationship.

...That when making our bed unasked, thus earning unexpected brownie points, it is mandatory, nay compulsory, to put six pillows, a zillion cushions and a throw, back into their correct positions and format. Any deviations, however slight will be met with disdain and criticism of my bed-making skills. Also, it will be suggested that I practise and practise and practise, then practise some more, until I finally get it right. One good tip for all the trainee bedmakers out there, is to keep a handy tape measure by the side of the bed.

...That if you make the bed, do NOT put the cushions back any differently to normal. Most definitely, do not put the cushions in a new layout, this might include either a design on the floor, or building a world beating design on another bed in a different bedroom for a laugh. Others do not find it funny.

...That if I am making the bed whilst my wife is sitting at her dressing table, putting on her make-up and watching me in the mirror, I should make sure that I straighten the bottom sheet, otherwise my bed-making skills will be commented on.

...That when I hear my wife starting to put clean sheets and pillow cases on our bed, I should immediately stop whatever I am doing and rush to help her. During the time together, when I put my pyjamas back under my pillow, she will always ask me:

"Don't you want clean pyjamas with clean sheets?"

Work and

Hobbies...

I've learnt...

...That if I am watching television with my wife and offer to go and make the tea in the kitchen, I must not get distracted on the way by watching golf on the other television, return to the sitting room and sit down empty-handed. This will lead to the following conversation:

"You forgot, didn't you? You are useless where golf is concerned."

"I'll go and make it now."

...That when I acquire and build a lot of Lego, the first run of shelving I buy and put up to display my achievements is insufficient. More shelving must be purchased and installed at even greater cost. Building Lego is an expensive hobby.

...That if I say I am going to be home from playing golf by 2.00pm, but don't appear through the door until after 3.00pm I might be immediately shown the way back out.

...That if my wife says that she is going for lunch with her Mother and Sister and invites me along to join them, it would be better to say:

"Yes, I'll come, I'd love to join you, that would be great," instead of "I'm sorry, I'm busy, I have golf practise." Especially when it is raining.

...That it is not a good idea to sit and watch sport for three hours whilst my wife hares around the house doing all sorts of chores, including three loads of washing. I should at

least go and get the empty washing basket
to save her one trip upstairs.

...That it is not a good idea to turn on the
kitchen sink tap, leave it running, and go and
sit down and watch golf. A short while later
I will be likely to hear:

"Did you mean to leave the kitchen tap
running?" This will be followed up swiftly by,
"How would you survive if you lived on your
own?" The only positive is that the sink

overflow pipe will save me from certain death.

...That if I am out playing golf with my besties and my wife is also out with her friends on the golf course, and that the holes we are both playing run parallel with each other, I should not march over to my wife and her friends and suggest that they speed up their play as they are playing slowly. Neither should I, especially against the advice of my besties, tell my wife and friends that they are holding up everyone around them. I could find that, on reaching the clubhouse later, and expecting to join my wife for lunch, I am politely informed that she went straight home after finishing her round of golf. I could also find that I am met with a force of nature on reaching home that is unimaginable. Furthermore, I could also find that I am grounded for a week, with my mobile telephone impounded, thus ceasing all communication with my besties, and all enjoyable and pleasurable marital activities will become a distant memory for many weeks. My wife will also communicate to my besties that I will not be playing golf for at least a month.[7]

...That if I use my wife's make-up tweezers to build Lego, I must BE SURE to put them back in the multi-coloured make-up bag on the dressing-table.

...That if I go to the office and tell my wife that I will be home at a certain time, IT IS BEST TO BE HOME AT THAT TIME! Otherwise, I will receive a telephone call, which will be broadcast if I speak to my wife on speakerphone, meaning my colleagues in the office will hear a conversation that goes something like this:

"Where the **** are you? You said you would be home two hours ago, and now we are thirty minutes late for the restaurant!" My colleagues will collapse with howls of laughter and then immediately set about helping me draft a suitable lockdown passage for the following day.

...That there is an order of those who must be consulted with when organising a game of golf. The first is my wife. The second is my golf besties. My wife will always overrule my besties. It is one of those facts of life. However, once out with my besties life takes a different turn for a few hours.

Christmas etc...

I've learnt...

...That if my wife asks me to buy Christmas wrapping paper on the way home from the office, and I walk in empty-handed, I should not say that I visited three shops without success. When pressed, I will have to admit that the three places visited were two garages and a pet shop. All excuses such as having to park, pay, walk miles, to visit a gift shop will fall on deaf ears, and I will be despatched to the proper gift shop the following day.

...That I must not leave the Lego Christmas catalogue lying around after dinner. My wife will start flicking through it and come across Harry Potter's Diagon Alley. She will jokingly suggest that I buy it whilst being aghast at the price, even more so on finding out I have already purchased it. "You spent HOW much?"

...That when in mid-November, my wife asks me to write out all the Christmas cards and I agree, I need to make sure that I have written them all out by the beginning of December. If I am late doing this and suddenly remember in mid-December, then alas, I will find my wife will have written them herself and I will be chastised for getting her hopes up again in vain.

...That when I ask my wife if I may play golf on Christmas Eve, and she says yes, she really means no, and I should know this. I should also know and remember that there will be a house to clean, ready for Christmas Day.

...That when I thought my wife and I had agreed that we would exchange small Christmas presents this year, I will be reminded that I got that completely wrong and imagined it when she surprises me with the Lego Tree House on Christmas Day.

...That if my company very kindly gives me a John Lewis voucher for Christmas, my wife will happen upon it and acquire something that she will say is for both of us, when really, it is for her. My dreams of new golf equipment will be but a far and distant memory. When six paintings arrive, I will quietly be very pleased at her choice and use of my gift voucher.

...That when I have already finished my Easter egg and my wife utters the immortal words:

"Now, this is my Easter Egg" she really does mean it. Going against these words is not advisable. Also, when she discovers her egg is somewhat diminished in size and the wrapper has been tampered with, severe retribution will come my way. No amount of placating offers, including multiple boxes of expensive chocolates, will replace the loss of her Easter Egg.

Wise Words...

I've learnt...

...That before choosing a life partner, pet or deciding to have a child, take a moment to think about it before you commit to something this momentous. Think how you might feel about any of the above if you were to be shut in the house with them, with no escape, for nearly a year. Failure to explore and consider this eventuality may induce mild hysteria and hostile feelings should the circumstances actually arise.

And...

...That you absolutely should not 'quaff' a bottle of Rioja and then agree to rescue a dog that you have been warned is certifiably mentally excitable and as a result, has had four homes in their one short year of life on this planet. Such an action will result in you becoming deeply attached to said dog before the realisation hits you that your carpets, furniture, and relationships with neighbours are ruined. Also, any hopes of peaceful dog walks for the next 15-20 years will be scuppered. However, your life will be deeply enriched and fulfilled by the devoted and unconditional love she shows you. The rest of the problems will pale into insignificance.[8]

...That my wife is always right, most of the time.

...That the first question I ask my wife each day is always:

"How did you sleep last night?"

Followed by the second question, which is always:

"What are you doing today?"

The third is always:

"What shall we have for dinner tonight?"

Sometimes there is a fourth question:

"What day is it?"

...That going forward and from here on in, to ask my wife to proof-read 'What I've Learnt in Lockdown,' so that if the content offends, she can take the blame...

...That there are some powers greater than others... one is my wife. Another is 'The Few'.

...That it is simply best to say yes to everything, whatever the question. Life is easier and less painful, my wife remains calm and content and our relationship continues on an even and happy keel.

...That if you can do it, just do it. (Remember who said that?) Do not wait to be asked, do not expect thanks, do not expect praise, and do not expect a hug. Others will quietly and silently appreciate your actions. If you do not do it, someone else will have to do it, and you have no idea where this will lead, until it is maybe too late.

...That the importance and value in true friendships is unquantifiable, as in the connection provided by Zoom.

Also...

...That no-one is ever late for a Zoom meeting!

Most importantly of all, I've learnt...

...That my wife is always there for me.

So there you have it. Some of the things that have happened to me during lockdown. I have been asked how true these 'What I've Learnt in Lockdown' passages really are. Have these things really happened? I will let you, dear reader, be the judge of that! Even if I have elaborated some incidences a bit, all of them could have easily happened. Maybe they all did!

In closing, it is worth saying that my lovely and long-suffering wife Karen had full knowledge of my musings, though not necessarily every daily publication.

How did she know? Well, one Friday we were out to dinner with friends, and I was telling them about the daily bulletins that I had been sending to my work colleagues since March 23rd... My secret was out!

Postscript

As this book goes to print, along with you, I find myself back in lockdown. Chris de Burgh is again playing loudly in my office, much to my wife's consternation. She is fed up with Chris (sorry Chris), but I still love listening to him and always will.

In 37 years, the one thing we do not have in common is our taste in music. My wife is convinced that I am stuck in a musical time warp and have never left the 60s and 70s and 80s.

On January 5th I re-started my daily writings for the third time, sending out bulletins to my eighty or so work colleagues who were now working from home again. Many of them were on their own.

I opened with the following words:

'You know, in many ways, it is good to be back; to know that you are out there and reading my musings. Well, I hope you are. It is good to know I am not alone. I always feel connected with you when I press 'send' and for that, I thank you from the bottom of my heart.'

Connection is what this book was born out of. Connection, company, and knowing that friends, colleagues and others are out there in the ether, and that whilst we cannot see each other, we are not alone. There is always someone there for us whatever our circumstances.

I hope and pray that the vaccinations quickly become available for us all and that life will return to normal.

A Note from Karen...

Who would have guessed on March 23rd last year that our three-week lockdown would dominate our lives for the rest of the year? Not us. Chris duly packed up a few files and essentials from his office and re-located it to our kitchen table. After three days of me creeping around every time he 'Zoomed' a client, I threw the rubber gloves down and insisted that this was not going to work. Something had to change. He then requisitioned a spare bedroom as his office, and has remained there ever since. The room is tiny, but he has managed to fit into it an electronic drum kit in one corner, a golf putting mat on the floor, and, thanks to the courtesy of our local handyman, two rows of shelves going around the room to house his growing lockdown obsession of building Lego, whilst listening to Chris de Burgh. In fact, everything that Chris does in that room is accompanied by Chris de Burgh on repeat. Thankfully I can shut the door or drown it out with something more to my taste. (Sorry C.d.B.)

So, this room which you could hardly fit a single bed in before, is now his office-cum-drumming-cum-Lego-building-cum-golf putting room. I'm not sure Chris de Burgh isn't living up there too? At least he is out of the kitchen!

Chris loves mentoring and helping people. When we were all told to work from home he was very aware that a lot of his work colleagues, particularly the younger ones were not as lucky as he was in having space and human contact. He would have weekly team meetings which were and still are about connecting people. Not about sales or in fact anything company based. Just chatting, funny stories and eventually, what he had learnt in lockdown.

It's a funny thing when you have lived with someone for over thirty-six years and only now do you really find out what they are like to live with. A lot of what Chris has learnt in lockdown should not have come as a surprise to him. I'm pretty certain that most have been mentioned at least once before. A lot of what he has learnt I'm sure you will recognise. I'm also sure that I too am not the easiest person to live with, because I haven't found it easy.

No-one knows how long we are going to have to continue with this way of living, but as of now we do at least have hope and a way out. We cannot continue to live with lockdowns, however much we may learn from them. There is one thing I am sure of. However mad he may get me (or I him) I would not wish to share lockdown with anyone else!

*

Acknowledgements

My sincere thanks to my good friend of thirty years, Mike Moore. I owe you a huge debt of gratitude in guiding me to your good friend Lyn Halvorsen, herself an author in her own right. Lyn I thank you for the many hours you spent putting the draft manuscript of my book together, and for putting up with my constant additions, and your patience. Your input was unquantifiable in critiquing my words and advising on layout and content. The final manuscript only exists because of your expertise and knowledge. You then took many of my passages and brought them to life with your wonderful and funny illustrations, many of them showing actual events.

To Richard Bevan, of Polarity Publishing. Thank you, Richard, for your advice and guidance and for teaching me everything that I didn't know about self-publishing. Together, you and Lyn have been invaluable in turning my musings into a collective written reality.

To Maisie and Tiggy, my two Norfolk Terriers, 'my girls', for sitting by my side for hours, and keeping me company whilst I wrote.

To my two sons, Thomas and Joshua, you didn't do a lot, but the approaches you have to life were my inspiration to put pen to paper.

Besides my wife, I owe my continuing sanity through lockdown to the support of Chris de Burgh. Chris, your music has been my daily companion in the office, gym and when cooking, and played at high volume. Thank you.

To our many wine and food suppliers, thank you for keeping us sustained. With special thanks to The Grocer in Old Amersham, Lewis Twydle and Denbies Wine Estate Limited.

Without my original readers, my work colleagues, this book would never have seen the light of day. Thank you for putting up with my musings, letting me into your lives each day, for your contributions and for reading.

Thank you to my golf besties. We are always there for each other. Thank you for the chatter and your friendship in many unwritten ways.

Finally, to my wonderful wife Karen; without you there would be no book, and no reactions to my wayward actions that prompted, 'What I've Learnt in Lockdown'. You have taught me for over 37 years about life, marriage, where I go wrong, and have corrected me many times, sometimes more than once. You have guided and steered our marriage through ups and downs, and stood by me through both dark and light times. Not only that, you are the only person who could, would and has put up with me. No-one but you could have survived lockdown with me.

This book is about us. Without you, there is no us.

Thank you.

Biography

Chris Mellor was born in Edgware, North London and now lives in Amersham, Buckinghamshire with his wife and two Norfolk Terriers. He is still enjoying a four-decade career in Financial Services, and like many, with recent time on his hands, started recording his lockdown experiences to fill the time, whilst also discovering that he was an Adult Fan of Lego. This was instigated by his wife, who gave him a set of Lego one Christmas, and therefore, only has herself to blame. Filling his time with golf, his family and his dogs, this is Chris's first step into the world of authorship.

Chris can be contacted at
chrismellor14@hotmail.com

References

1. Andrew Aitken Rooney

https://en.wikipedia.org/wiki/Andy_Rooney

Friends and colleagues have kindly contributed some of their own quotations, and they are listed here with my special thanks:

2. Katie Melling
3. Kayleigh Kennington
4. Elisabeth Groves
5. Laura Niven
6. Doug Muirhead
7. Cathy and Frank Ginger
8. Elisabeth Groves

Printed in Great Britain
by Amazon

58632222R00061